Developing Science Language

for
Physical Processes
with
6–7
year olds

Charlotte Clarke

Published by Scholastic Ltd,
Villiers House,
Clarendon Avenue,
Leamington Spa,
Warwickshire CV32 5PR
Visit our website at www.scholastic.co.uk

Printed by Alden Group Ltd, Oxford

© 2001 Scholastic Ltd
Text © Charlotte Clarke 2001

1234567890 1234567890

AUTHOR
Charlotte Clarke

LITERACY CONSULTANT
Gill Matthews

EDITOR
Joel Lane

ASSISTANT EDITOR
Roanne Davis

SERIES DESIGNER
Rachael Hammond

COVER PHOTOGRAPH
© Stockbyte

ILLUSTRATIONS
Ann Kronheimer

British Library Cataloguing-in-Publication Data
A catalogue record for this book is available from the British Library.

ISBN 0-439-01873-0

Designed using Adobe Pagemaker

The right of Charlotte Clarke to be identified as the Author of this work has been asserted by her in accordance with the Copyright, Designs and Patents Act 1988.

All rights reserved. This book is sold subject to the condition that it shall not, by way of trade or otherwise, be lent, hired out or otherwise circulated without the publisher's prior consent in any form of binding or cover other than that in which it is published and without a similar condition, including this condition, being imposed upon the subsequent purchaser.

No part of this publication may be reproduced, stored in a retrieval system, or transmitted, in any form or by any means, electronic, mechanical, photocopying, recording or otherwise, without the prior permission of the publisher. This book remains copyright, although permission is granted to copy those pages indicated as photocopiable for classroom distribution and use only in the school which has purchased the book, or by the teacher who has purchased this book and in accordance with the CLA licensing agreement. Photocopying permission is given for purchasers only and not for borrowers of books from any lending service.

CONTENTS

5 Introduction
6 Word list

7 Using and misusing electricity ......*(information text)*

8 Using and misusing electricity questions ......*(lower level)*
9 Using and misusing electricity questions ......*(higher level)*
10 Mains or battery ......*(chart completion)*
11 Switching on ......*(description)*
12 What's the problem ......*(matching pictures and writing)*
14 Electricity is useful ......*(labelling)*
15 Spot the danger ......*(describing)*
16 Electricity in the classroom ......*(labelling)*

17 Making a circuit ......*(instruction text)*

18 Making a circuit questions ......*(lower level)*
19 Making a circuit questions ......*(higher level)*
20 Which ones work? ......*(labelling)*
21 Which ones work? 2 ......*(describing)*
22 Using buzzers and motors ......*(labelling)*

23 Pushes and pulls ......*(recount/report)*

24 Pushes and pulls questions ......*(lower level)*
25 Pushes and pulls questions ......*(higher level)*
26 Cars ......*(sequencing)*
27 Cars 2 ......*(analysing graph)*
28 Forces words ......*(labelling)*

29 Speeding up and slowing down ......*(recount/report)*

30 Speeding up and slowing down questions ......*(lower level)*
31 Speeding up and slowing down questions ......*(higher level)*
32 Fast and slow book ......*(book making)*
33 Fast or slow? ......*(sequencing)*
34 Stopping and starting ......*(matching sentence starters and endings)*
35 More speeding up and slowing down ......*(describing)*
36 Toy cars ......*(cloze and describing)*

CONTENTS

37 Making sounds ......(recount/report)
    38 Making sounds questions ......(lower level)
    39 Making sounds questions ......(higher level)
    40 Sound makers ......(table completion)
    41 High and low ......(labelling)
    42 Sound words ......(text marking)
    43 What does it sound like? ......(describing)
    44 Where do you hear these sounds? ......(table completion)

45 Hearing sounds ......(advertisement)
    46 Hearing sounds questions ......(lower level)
    47 Hearing sounds questions ......(higher level)
    48 String telephones ......(writing instructions)
    49 Sound travels ......(labelling and true/false statements)
    50 Ear trumpets ......(sequencing)

51 Light and dark ......(description/recount)
    52 Light and dark questions ......(lower level)
    53 Light and dark questions ......(higher level)
    54 Light sources ......(labelling)
    55 Warning lights ......(labelling)
    56 Light sources game ......(round-the-class card game)

57 Day and night ......(information text)
    58 Day and night questions ......(lower level)
    59 Day and night questions ......(higher level)
    60 In the sky ......(matching pictures and labels)
    61 Morning, midday, evening and night ......(describing)
    62 Day and night dictionary ......(dictionary making)
    64 Shadows in the day and at night ......(describing)

INTRODUCTION

Children often struggle to remember science words. Sometimes the words seem strange or unusual, and sometimes the words we use in science have other meanings. Think about these science words: *force, material, property, sink*. If you ask a child what these words mean, you are likely to get responses such as: 'If you force someone to do something, it's not very nice'; 'My coat is made of material'; 'My things are my property'; 'The sink is where we wash up after painting'. But when children go into science lessons, we sometimes assume that they already understand a 'force' to be a push or a pull, a 'material' to be any substance, a 'property' to be how a material behaves, and 'sink' to be what some things do in water.

Scientific language

This series aims to give children practice in using science words, both through science activities and in 'real life' contexts, so that they become familiar with the scientific meanings of these words. Use of correct scientific vocabulary is essential for high attainment in SATs tests. The QCA *Scheme of Work for Science* (DfEE) for Key Stages 1 and 2 in England suggests examples of vocabulary for each of its units; although these books are not divided into exactly the same topics, the QCA vocabulary and its progressive introduction are used as the basis for the word selection here.

The science covered is divided into units based on topics from the national curricula for England, Wales, Scotland and Northern Ireland. In this book, the science is drawn from the 'Physical processes' statements for ages 6–7 relating to electricity, forces, light (including the Sun, the Moon and daylight) and sound. The series of boxed letters at the bottom of each page shows in which curriculum documents the focus of each activity occurs. For example, for the text on page 17, the boxes E NI W S indicate that the activity focuses on a topic from the National Curricula for England and for Wales.

Science and literacy

The National Literacy Strategy for England suggests teaching objectives and gives examples of the types of activities that children should encounter during each year of primary school. This book uses many of these techniques for developing children's understanding and use of scientific language. The activities are mainly intended for use in science time, as they have been written with science learning objectives in mind. However, some of the activities could be used in literacy time. Science texts have already been published for use in literacy time, but many of them use science content appropriate for older children.

During literacy time you need to be focusing on language skills, not teaching new science. It is with this in mind that these sheets, drawing from age-appropriate science work, have been produced. It is also suggested that these sheets are used in literacy time only after the science content has been introduced in science time.

The series focuses on paper-based activities to develop scientific language, but it is hoped that teachers might use some of the ideas in planning practical science activities.

About this book

Each unit in this book begins with a non-fiction text that introduces some key scientific vocabulary. The key words are highlighted by bold type. The texts cover a range of non-fiction genres.

Following this text are two comprehension activities that help children to identify and understand the key words (and a range of additional science words). They are pitched at two levels:

 for older or more able children

 for younger or less able children.

Although the comprehension activities are designed to be used mainly during science time, you may wish to use the texts as examples of non-fiction texts in the literacy hour. The comprehension pages contain two or three types of question (a change of icon indicates a change in the type of question):

 The answer can be found in the text.

 Children will need to think about the answer. These questions usually elicit science understanding beyond what the text provides.

 An activity aimed at developing children's literacy skills. These are optional extension activities for individual or group work, with teacher support if necessary.

Following the comprehension pages in each unit are activities aimed at developing children's understanding and use of the key vocabulary. Strategies used include completion of charts, description, matching pictures and writing, labelling, sequencing, analysing graphs and tables, making books, matching sentence starters to endings, cloze text, text marking, writing instructions, identifying true and false statements, a round-the-class card game and making dictionaries.

WORD LIST

Electricity words
- battery
- break
- bulb
- bulb holder
- buzzer
- circuit
- crocodile clip
- danger
- electricity
- mains electricity
- metal
- motor
- plastic
- plug
- power station
- pylon
- socket
- switch
- wire

Forces words
- easy
- fast
- force
- hard
- harder
- pull
- push
- slow
- speed
- start
- stop
- twist

Sound words
- bang
- drum
- ears
- guitar
- hear
- high
- loud
- low
- noise
- pluck
- quiet
- rattle
- shake
- silence
- silent
- soft
- sound
- sound maker

Light words
- afternoon
- black
- bright
- clouds
- colour
- dark
- darker
- day
- daytime
- dim
- evening
- light
- light source
- midday
- Moon
- morning
- night
- reflect
- safe
- see
- shadow
- shiny
- sky
- stars
- Sun
- warning
- white

Using and misusing electricity

Electricity is made in **power stations**. Wires carry it to our homes and schools. Some wires are under the ground and others are high up on **pylons**. It is very dangerous to climb on pylons, because the electricity could give you a shock big enough to kill you.

Electricity is very useful. The electricity used in our homes is called **mains electricity**. Things such as kettles and toasters are plugged into the mains electricity. Sometimes **batteries** are used for electricity. A small radio may work using batteries.

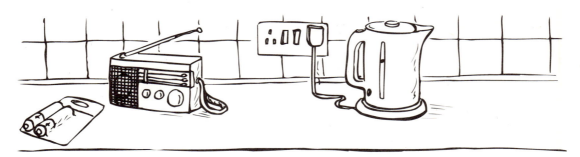

Electricity is dangerous, but if we are careful we can use it safely in our homes. Always make sure that your hands are dry when you use electricity. **Plug** in electrical things carefully. Hold the **plastic** part of the plug – do not touch the **metal** parts. Push the plug right into the **socket**. Now it is safe to switch on.

If a plug is broken, tell an adult straight away. Never put your fingers into a socket. Never put anything except a plug into a socket.

Using and misusing electricity

1. Where is electricity made? _____

2. How does electricity get to our homes?
   _____

3. Why is it dangerous to climb electricity pylons?
   _____

4. Make a list of ten things in your house that use electricity.
   _____
   _____

5. When you are using electricity, make sure your hands are
   _____

6. Which part of a plug should you hold? _____

7. What should you do if a plug is broken? _____
   _____

8. Why is it dangerous to put a knife into an electric socket?
   _____

9. Draw a sign to stop people climbing up pylons.

Make a poster warning children not to play with plugs and sockets. Include three things to remember when you are using a plug.

DEVELOPING SCIENCE LANGUAGE for Physical Processes with 6–7 year olds

Using and misusing electricity

1. Where is electricity made? _____

2. Electricity comes to our homes through _____.

3. The wires are held high up on pylons. Draw a pylon.

4. Is it safe to climb up a pylon?

    _____

5. Make a list of ten things in your home that need electricity to make them work.

    1. Kettle
    2. _____
    3. _____
    4. _____
    5. _____
    6. _____
    7. _____
    8. _____
    9. _____
    10. _____

For questions 6–8, tick the correct box.

6. When you are using electricity, your hands should be   dry ○   wet ○

7. When you use a plug, you should hold the part made from   plastic ○   metal ○

8. Look at this plug.

    It is safe to use. ○   It is not safe – tell an adult. ○

Make a poster warning children not to play with plugs and sockets. Include three things to remember when you are using a plug.

DEVELOPING SCIENCE LANGUAGE for Physical Processes with 6–7 year olds

Mains or battery?

Some things use mains electricity. You have to plug them in to make them work.
Other things use batteries.
Some things can use either mains electricity or batteries.

Write the name to show where each thing should go in the diagram.

radio | TV | camera | washing machine | watch
torch | toaster | kettle | personal stereo | computer

DEVELOPING SCIENCE LANGUAGE for Physical Processes with 6–7 year olds

Switching on

Electricity is very useful.

What happens when you switch each thing on?
Write in the boxes to explain what happens.

1 What's the problem?

Cut out the cards on these two pages.
Match the pictures with the writing.

What's the problem?

If you switch the toaster on when your hands are wet, you could get an electric shock.	The boy could get a big shock if he puts the knife in the socket.
Climbing a pylon is very silly. It can cause you to get a huge shock from the cable.	The wires are coming loose from the plug. You could get an electric shock from the wires.
If the sign says 'DANGER', you should never go inside.	Electricity and water don't mix.
Plugging too many things into one socket is dangerous.	Adults should make sure they unplug electrical items before they try to repair them.

Electricity is useful

Each of these things needs electricity to make it work.
Some of the things get hot. They give out **heat**.
Some of the things make **light**.
Some of the things make **sound**.

In the space under each picture, write what you want the thing to make when you switch it on. Choose **heat**, **light** or **sound**.

toaster	cassette player	lamp	telephone
	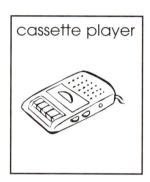		
television	kettle	CD player	hairdryer
			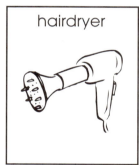
light	heater	computer	doorbell
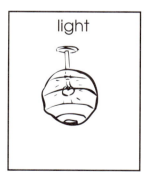			

Draw three more things you know that use electricity to make heat, light and sound.

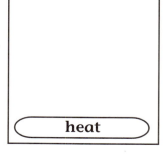 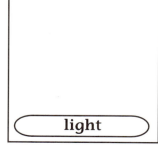 

heat	light	sound

Spot the danger

Each of these pictures shows something that makes heat or sound. Can you spot the danger in each picture?
Write about the danger, using some of the words in the box.

speakers	burn	danger	damage	quiet
dangerous	heat	sound	man	child
ears	loud	hot	touch	

Before we had electric heaters and gas fires, people made fires by burning wood or coal to keep warm. Some people still like to have a fire. This can be dangerous because

_____
_____
_____

Some people have an electric cooker. This can be dangerous because

_____
_____
_____

These people are at a concert. The music is very, very loud.

_____
_____
_____

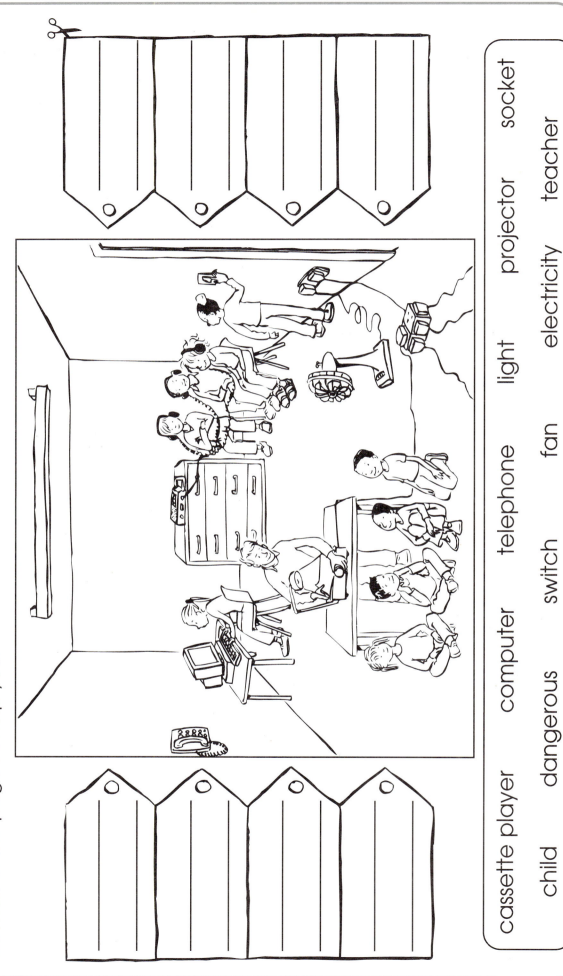

Making a circuit

Here are some instructions for making a simple **circuit**.

What you need

a **bulb** in a **holder**   3 **wires** with **crocodile clips**

 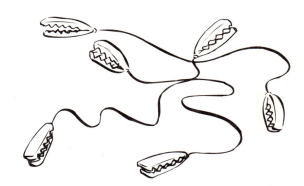

a **switch**   a **battery**

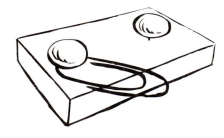 

What you do

1. Clip one end of a wire to a screw on the bulb holder.

2. Clip the other end of the wire to one of the metal strips on top of the battery.

3. Clip another wire to the other metal strip on the battery.

4. Clip the other end of this wire to one pin on the switch.

5. Connect the other pin on the switch to the bulb holder with the last wire.

6. Close the switch. The light should come on.

Making a circuit

1. What is the name of each of these things?

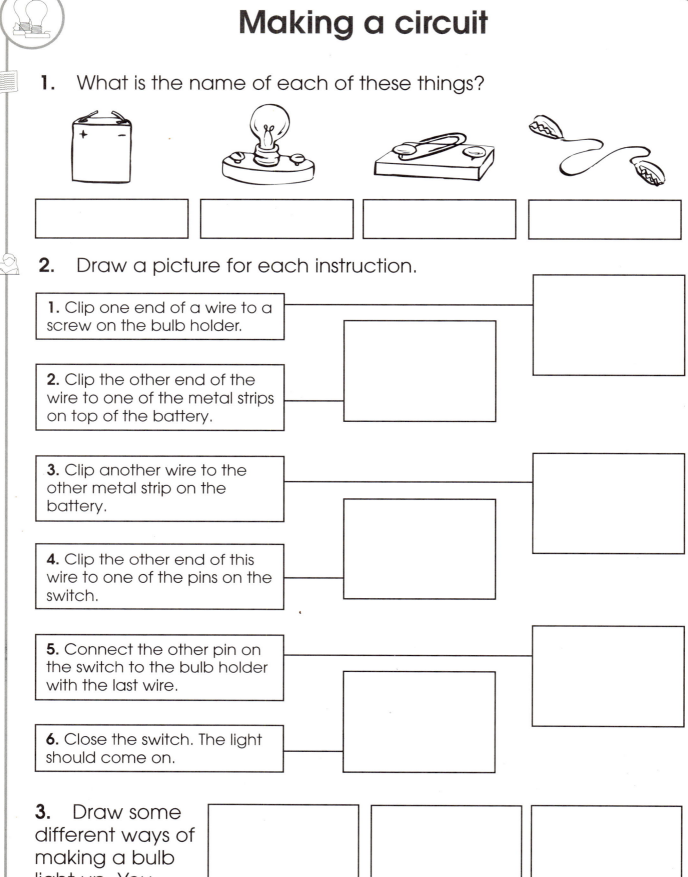

2. Draw a picture for each instruction.

   1. Clip one end of a wire to a screw on the bulb holder.

   2. Clip the other end of the wire to one of the metal strips on top of the battery.

   3. Clip another wire to the other metal strip on the battery.

   4. Clip the other end of this wire to one of the pins on the switch.

   5. Connect the other pin on the switch to the bulb holder with the last wire.

   6. Close the switch. The light should come on.

3. Draw some different ways of making a bulb light up. You may need to try out your ideas.

DEVELOPING SCIENCE LANGUAGE for Physical Processes with 6–7 year olds

Making a circuit

1. What is the name of each of these things?
How many of each do you need to make a circuit?

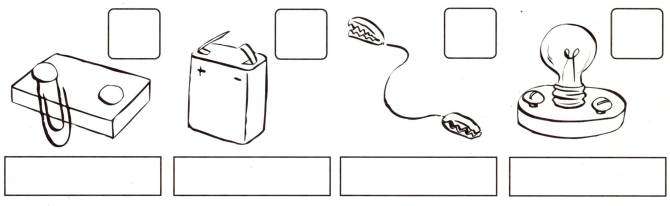

2. Cut out the writing and the pictures.
Match the pictures to the instructions.

1. Clip one end of a wire to a screw on the bulb holder.

2. Clip the other end of the wire to one of the metal strips on top of the battery.

3. Clip another wire to the other metal strip on the battery.

4. Clip the other end of this wire to one of the pins on the switch.

5. Connect the other pin on the switch to the bulb holder with the last wire.

6. Close the switch. The light should come on.

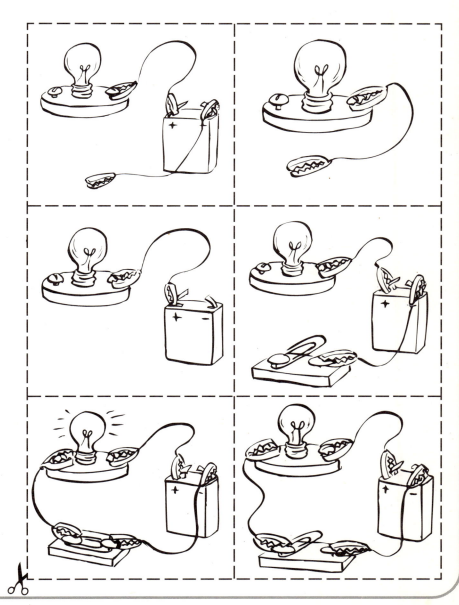

Which ones work?

Tick the boxes to show which lights will come on.
You will need to look at the pictures very carefully.

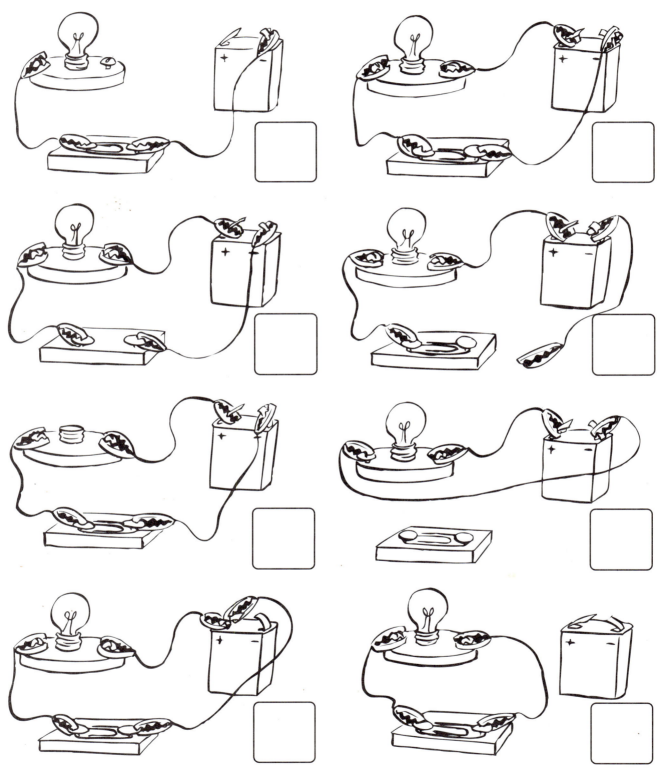

Draw a circle on each picture of a circuit that will not work to show where the problem is.

Which ones work?

The bulbs in these circuits do not work. Why not?
Write under each picture. Use the words in the box to help you.

> wire   circuit   battery   connected
> bulb   crocodile clip   paper clip

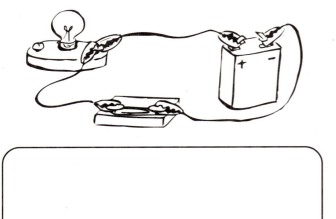

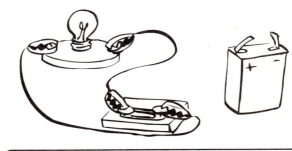

Using buzzers and motors

A **buzzer** makes a noise. This is a circuit with a buzzer in it. When you close the switch, the buzzer buzzes.

Label the circuit using these words:

switch   battery   wire
crocodile clip   buzzer

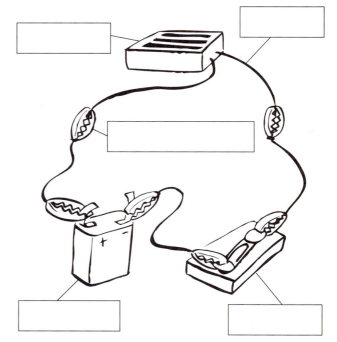

When the switch is open, we say there is a **break** in the circuit.

Does the buzzer work when there is a break in the circuit?

yes   no

motor

A **motor** turns around when you connect it to a battery. This motor is making a toy roundabout work.

Which of these needs a motor to make it work? Tick the pictures of things that need a motor.

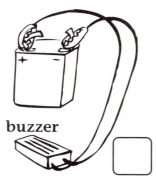

Clown toy with spinning bow-tie   Toy spin-dryer made from paper and plastic cups   Toy doorbell   Toy house with lights inside

Pushes and pulls

A group of children were learning about **forces**. A **force** is a **push** or a **pull**. The children were trying to fit a foam ball into different containers.

This is what they wrote:

First we tried to put the ball into a bowl.
We **pushed** it in.
It went in **easily**.

Then we tried to get the ball out. We had to **pull** it to get it out. It was **easy** to **pull** out.

Then we put the ball into a mug.
We had to **push** it **hard** to make it fit.

It was **harder** to **push** it into the mug than into the bowl.

It was **harder** to **pull** it out too.

Then we tried to **push** the ball into a small cup.
We **pushed** it really **hard**, but it wouldn't go in.

Our teacher could make it go into the cup.
She could **push** much **harder** than we could.

We had to **pull** it very **hard** to get it out of the cup.

Photocopiable

Pushes and pulls

 1. What is a force? _____

_____

2. What were the children doing? _____

_____

 3. Was the ball easy or hard to push into

- the bowl?
- the mug?
- the cup?

 4. What did the children have to do to get the ball out of each container? _____

_____

5. Tick which needed the biggest force: pulling the ball out of the

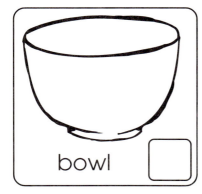  

 6. Why could the teacher make the ball go into the cup when the children could not? _____

_____

DEVELOPING SCIENCE LANGUAGE for Physical Processes with 6–7 year olds

Pushes and pulls

1. A force is a _____ or a _____.

2. To find out about forces, the children tried to put a _____ into different-sized containers.

For questions 3–5, circle the correct answer.

3. When they pushed the ball into the bowl,

   it was **easy / hard**.

4. When they pushed the ball into the mug,

   it was **easy / hard**.

5. When they pushed the ball into the cup,

   it was **easy / hard / very hard**.

6. To get the ball out of each container, the children had to

   _____

   _____

   _____ .

7. Could the children make the ball go into the cup? _____

8. Could the teacher make the ball go into the cup? _____

9. The children could not get the ball into the cup because

the cup was too small / they could not push hard enough.

10. The teacher could get the ball into the cup because

the cup was bigger / she could push hard enough.

DEVELOPING SCIENCE LANGUAGE for Physical Processes with 6–7 year olds

Photocopiable

1 Cars

Some children were rolling toy cars down a slope to find out which one would go the furthest. They wrote about what they did, but their sentences have got muddled up. Put their sentences into the correct order.

We let the cars go.

We waited until the cars stopped.

Then we held the toy cars at the top of the slope.

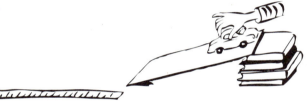

Then we put a tape-measure at the bottom of the slope.

First, we made a slope by putting one end of a tray on a pile of books.

To finish, we measured how far each car had gone.

The cars rolled down the slope.

Cars

The children cut pieces of string to show how far the cars had gone. They stuck the string to a big sheet of paper.

How far the car went (cm)

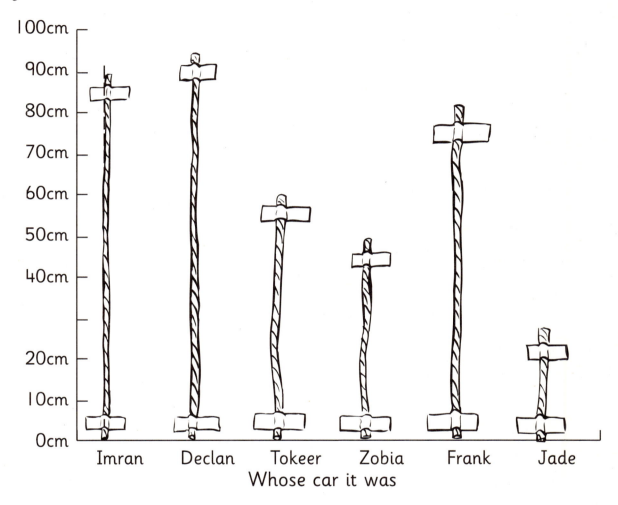

Whose car it was

1. How far did Imran's car go? _____

2. How far did Zobia's car go? _____

3. One number is missing on the graph.

   What should it be? _____

4. Whose car went the furthest? _____

5. Whose car went the shortest distance? _____

Forces words

Use the forces words in the box to describe what each person is doing. Write the correct word under each picture.

dragging	stretching	twisting	lifting
kicking	blowing	sucking
pushing	throwing	pulling

 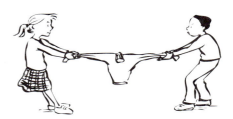

 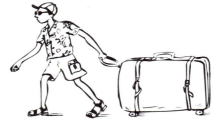 

Speeding up and slowing down

Amy went to the park with her mum. She went on her bike. At the park, she rode her bike around the playground. The playground was smooth, so the bike went quite **fast**. Amy was going so fast that she could not **stop**. She crashed into a bench.

Then Amy tried to ride her bike on the grass. It was hard to push the pedals round on the grass. The bike went very **slowly**.

Then Amy tried to ride her bike on the path. The path was made from small stones, and Amy could not make the bike **start** at all.

Then Amy rode down the hill. The bike went faster and faster. It **speeded up**.

Finally, she tried to ride up the hill. It was hard work. If she didn't push on the pedals, the bike **slowed down**. Amy was very tired when she got home.

Photocopiable

Speeding up and slowing down

1. Why did Amy's bike go fast in the playground? _____
   _____

2. Why did Amy's bike stop in the playground? _____
   _____

3. Write these words in the correct place in the table.

   - on the playground
   - on the grass
   - on the path
   - downhill
   - uphill

easy to ride	hard to ride

4. How could Amy make her bike go faster?   Tick the correct boxes.

   Ride uphill. ☐
   Ride downhill. ☐
   Ride on the grass. ☐
   Ride on the path. ☐
   Pedal harder. ☐
   Ride on the playground. ☐
   Ride on rough stones. ☐

5. How could Amy make her bike go more slowly?

   Ride uphill. ☐
   Ride downhill. ☐
   Ride on the grass. ☐
   Put her feet on the ground. ☐
   Stop pedalling. ☐

Have you ever ridden on a bike or a trike, or in a toy car with pedals? Write about your ride.

Speeding up and slowing down

To answer these questions, circle the correct words.

1. The playground was **rough / smooth**,

   so Amy's bike could go **fast / slowly**.

2. Amy's bike stopped in the playground because it crashed into a _____.

3. Was it easy or hard to ride the bike

   - on the playground?   **easy / hard**
   - on the grass?   **easy / hard**
   - on the path?   **easy / hard**
   - going down the hill?   **easy / hard**
   - going up the hill?   **easy / hard**

4. Will Amy go faster or slower?

faster / slower

faster / slower

faster / slower

faster / slower

Have you ever ridden on a bike or a trike, or in a toy car with pedals? Write about your ride.

Fast and slow book

Make a fast and slow book like this.

1. Fold a piece of paper in half.

2. Open it out.

3. Fold each side into the middle.

4. Write **fast** on one side and **slow** on the other side.

5. Cut out the pictures below and stick them in your fast and slow book.

6. Draw some more pictures of fast and slow things in your book.

			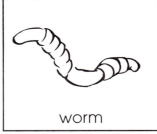
aeroplane	bird	baby	worm
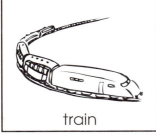			
train	bike	snail	motorbike

car	horse	person walking	person running

Fast or slow?

Here are some fast and slow words:

swim

drive

run   walk

ride   sit

crawl

fly

Put the words in order, starting with the fastest.

fastest
slowest

Tell your teacher why you put the words in this order.

Stopping and starting

Match the beginning of each sentence to the correct ending.

Beginning	Ending
To stop a bike,	it will slow down and then stop and then roll down again.
If you put a toy car on a slope and let go,	you need to push on the pedals.
To make a toy train start moving,	you need to put on the brakes.
To start a bike,	it will start moving down the slope.
If you roll a ball up a hill,	you kick it or roll it or throw it.
If you roll a toy car into a wall,	it will stop.
A football will not move unless	you need to push it.

Finish these sentences yourself.

If you roll a ball down a hill, _____

_____

To move a shopping trolley, _____

_____

More speeding up and slowing down

Look at these pictures. How could each thing be made to go faster?

toy car on ramp

supermarket trolley

car on motorway

_____
_____
_____
_____

Look at these pictures. How could each thing be made to go more slowly?

cars outside school

bike going down a hill

baby with truck of toy bricks

_____
_____
_____
_____

Toy cars

Use the words in the box to fill the gaps.
You will need to use each word once.

To start a toy car moving, you can push it or _____ it. If you push it gently, it will go _____. If you push it harder, it will go _____. If the toy car rolls into a wall, it will _____.

If you roll a toy car down a slope, it will _____ up. If you roll the car along the floor, it will _____ down and then _____.

| faster | slow | stop |
| stop | pull | speed | slowly |

Label these pictures. What are the children doing?

Making sounds

These children made some **sound makers**. They are making sounds with them to go with a story their teacher is reading.

Nadia has made a **drum** from an ice-cream tub. She **bangs** it to make a **noise**. It makes a **loud** sound. Rupe's sound maker is a **rattle**. It is a plastic bottle with beans inside. He **shakes** it to make a sound. Alice has made a **guitar** from elastic bands and a shoe box. She **plucks** the elastic bands to make sounds. The sounds of this guitar are quite **soft**. They are **quiet**. Some of the sounds the guitar makes are **high** sounds and some are **low** sounds. The children make the sounds as their teacher reads the story.

At the end of the story, the teacher wants **silence**. All the children stop making noises. There is no sound now. It is really quiet. It is **silent**.

Photocopiable

Making sounds

1. What sound makers did the children make?
   _____   _____   _____

2. What did Rupe make his sound maker from? _____
   _____

3. How does Nadia make a sound? _____

   How does Rupe make a sound? _____

   How does Alice make a sound? _____

4. Circle the correct word.

   Nadia's drum makes a **loud / quiet** noise.

   Alice's guitar makes a **loud / quiet** noise.

5. Another word for a quiet sound is a _____ sound.

6. Some sounds the guitar makes are high. Some are _____.

7. Write the names of some things you know that make quiet sounds. _____
   _____

8. Write the names of some things you know that make loud sounds. _____
   _____

9. At the end of the story, the teacher wanted silence. What is silence? _____

In a group, make a dictionary of the **bold words** on the 'Making sounds' sheet. Write down what each word means.

DEVELOPING SCIENCE LANGUAGE for Physical Processes with 6–7 year

Making sounds

1. Nadia made a _____. Rupe made a _____. Alice made a _____.

2. Nadia's drum was made from _____.

3. Nadia _____ her drum to make a sound.

4. Rupe _____ his rattle to make a sound.

5. Alice _____ her guitar to make a sound.

6. Nadia's drum makes a **loud / quiet** sound.

7. Alice's guitar makes a **loud / quiet** sound.

8. Another word for quiet is **loud / soft / high**.

9. Some sounds the guitar makes are high. Some are _____.

10. Tick the quiet sounds.

    aeroplane ☐
    train ☐
    wind ☐
    bee ☐
    dog barking ☐
    a door opening ☐
    beans cooking ☐
    disco ☐
    motorbike ☐

11. Which are sound words? Tick the correct boxes.

    sing ☐   push ☐
    cry ☐   shout ☐
    smell ☐   see ☐
    write ☐   walk ☐
    talk ☐

12. The teacher wanted silence. When it is silent, there is no _____.

In a group, make a dictionary of the **bold words** on the 'Making sounds' sheet. Write down what each word means.

Sound makers

shake	pluck
_____	_____
_____	_____

blow	bang
_____	_____
_____	_____

What do you do to each thing to make a sound?
Draw the sound makers and write their names in the correct boxes.

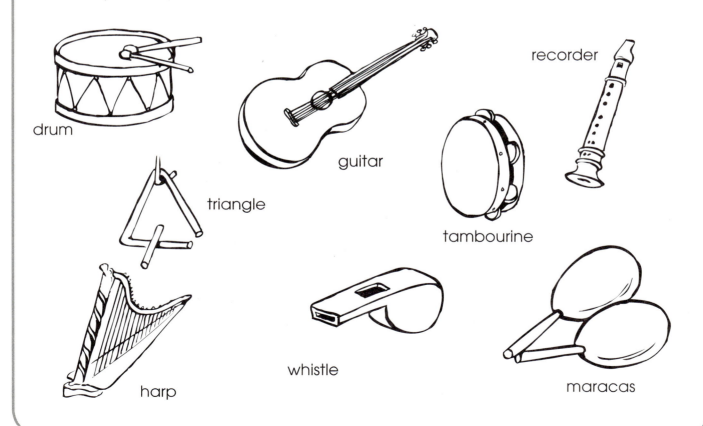

drum, guitar, recorder, triangle, tambourine, harp, whistle, maracas

High and low

Which of these make high sounds? Which make low sounds?
Do some make high sounds *and* low sounds?
Write **high** or **low** or **high and low** next to each picture.

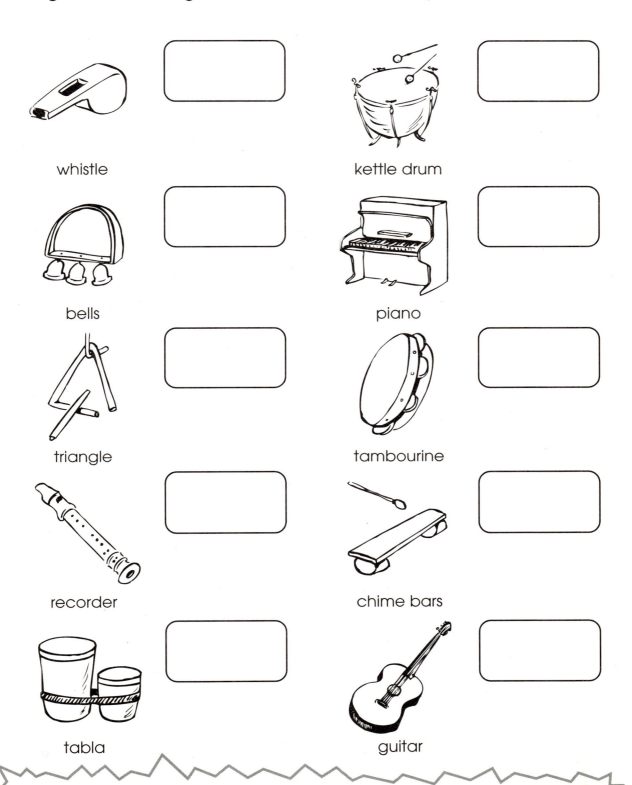

Be careful! **High** and **low** are not the same as **loud** and **quiet**.

Sound words

Read this piece of writing. Underline the names of things that **make** sounds in **blue**. Underline the words that **describe** sounds in **red**.

Class 2 went for a walk around the school. The children were listening for different sounds. First of all, they heard the fire alarm being tested. It made a very loud sound. Next, they heard the cook in the kitchen. She was banging saucepans. The sound was very loud. The children thought it was a horrible noise.

Then the children went outside. They could hear birds in the trees. The birds made quiet whistling sounds. The school was in the countryside. The children could hear sheep in the fields. The sheep sounded as if they were saying "Baaaa".

The older children came out to play. Some were shouting loudly and some were talking quietly.

At the end of playtime, the children heard a whistle. It sounded high and loud. When they heard the whistle, they went inside quietly. Mrs Jones, the caretaker, had her radio on. She was putting out tables for dinner. She banged the tables together and they made loud noises.

What does it sound like?

Write a sentence or two to go with each picture. You can use these words to help you.

loud	quiet	high	low	silent
blow	sing	pluck	talk	bang	noise
traffic	drum	guitar	recorder	sound

The drummer _____ the drum to make a _____ sound. The guitar player _____

Photocopiable

Where do you hear these sounds?

Do you hear these sounds at home? Do you hear them in the street?
Do you hear these sounds at school? Do you hear them in the countryside?

Cut out the pictures and stick them in the correct boxes.

At home	In the street
At school	In the countryside

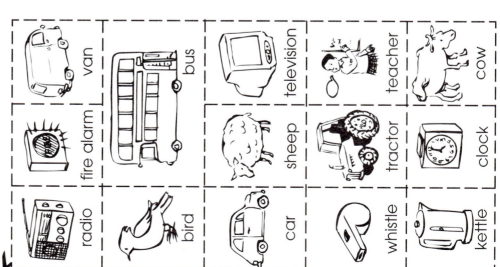

van, fire alarm, radio
bus, bird
television, sheep, car
teacher, lion, whistle
cow, tractor, clock, kettle

DEVELOPING SCIENCE LANGUAGE for Physical Processes with 6–7 year

Hearing sounds

FANTASTIC NEW HEARING AID

This is Bob. Bob cannot **hear** very well, because his **ears** were hurt in an accident. **Sounds** go into Bob's **ears**, but even very **loud** sounds seem **quiet** to him. He has tried a new hearing aid to help him hear better. Bob said:

Fantastic! The hearing aid is great. I can hear you talking. I can hear birds singing. I can hear so much better!

You wear the hearing aid in your ear. It works by making sounds **louder** inside your ear, so they are easier to hear.

Ask your doctor about the new hearing aid.

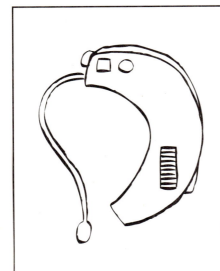

Clearasound

Photocopiable

Hearing sounds

  1. We hear with our _____.

  2. Bob cannot hear very well. What does that mean? _____
_____

3. What did Bob try to help him hear better? _____
_____

4. What does the hearing aid do to the sounds? _____
_____

5. What things did Bob say he can hear? _____
_____

  6. Imagine you were close to these things and could hear the sounds they made. Write their names in order, from the quietest to the loudest.

Quietest

_____

_____

_____

_____

_____

_____

_____

_____

Loudest

 dog barking
 bird singing
 aeroplane
 whistle
 train
 tap running
 lorry
 pop group
 wind blowing

Write a doctor's report on how the hearing aid has helped Bob.

DEVELOPING SCIENCE LANGUAGE for Physical Processes with 6–7 year year olds

Hearing sounds

 1. This is Bob. Draw an arrow to show where a sound goes when he hears it.

Circle the correct word.

2. We hear with our **eyes / arms / ears**.

3. Very loud sounds seem **loud / quiet** to Bob.

4. Bob's ears don't work very well, so he tried a new

_____ _____.

5. Tick the things that Bob said he could hear.

6. Write the names of these sounds in the correct boxes.

   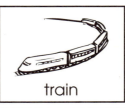 

Loud

Quiet

Write a doctor's report on how the hearing aid has helped Bob.

DEVELOPING SCIENCE LANGUAGE for Physical Processes with 6–7 year olds

String telephones

These children are using a string telephone to talk to each other. They made the telephone from plastic cups and string.

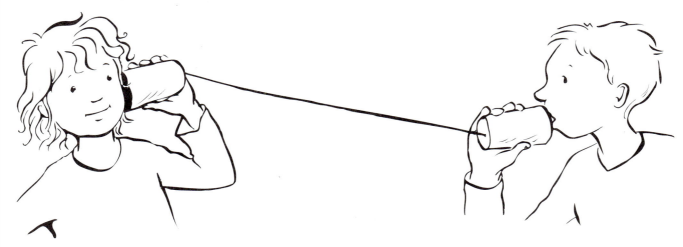

Write instructions for making and using a string telephone. You can use the words in the box to help you.

> plastic   cup   telephone   knot   tie
> ear   hole   scissors   two   talk   hold   cut
> one   mouth   tight   piece   string

Making a _____

You need: _____

_____

What to do
1. Make a hole in the bottom of each _____

_____

2. Then _____

_____

3. _____

_____

Sound travels

Label the picture by writing the numbers in the correct places.

1. The teacher put the clock in the middle of the playground.

2. The children walked away from the clock in all directions.

3. They listened carefully to the clock ticking as they walked.

4. When they could not hear the clock any more, they stopped walking.

5. This child's ears were the best. She could still hear the ticking when she was a long way from the clock.

Are these sentences true or false?

Sound travels from the clock in all directions. T F

Sound only travels in one direction from the clock. T F

The child whose hearing was best stopped nearest the clock. T F

The child whose hearing was best stopped furthest from the clock. T F

The sound of the clock is quietest near the clock. T F

The sound of the clock is loudest near the clock. T F

DEVELOPING SCIENCE LANGUAGE for Physical Processes with 6–7 year olds

Ear trumpets

Ear trumpets help you to hear by catching more sound. These children are making and testing ear trumpets. Their instructions have got mixed up.
Put the instructions in the correct order.

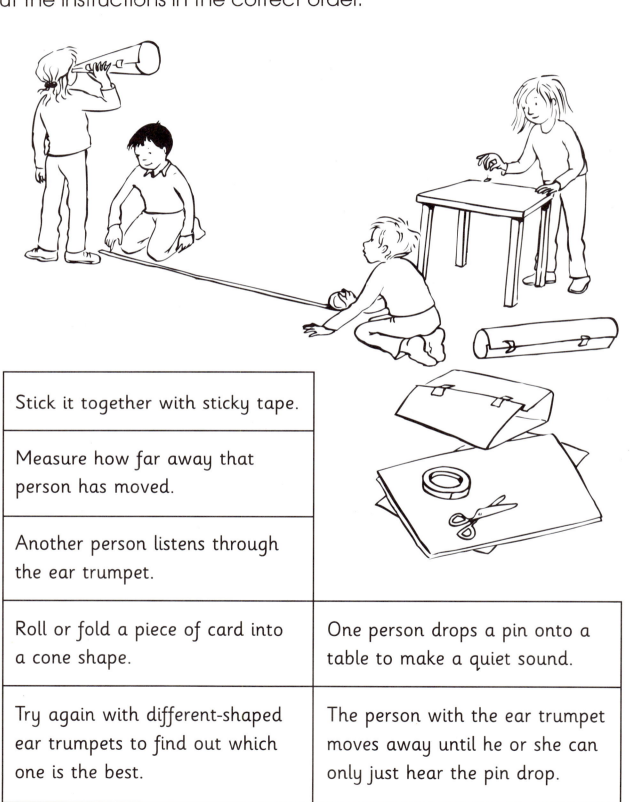

Stick it together with sticky tape.	
Measure how far away that person has moved.	
Another person listens through the ear trumpet.	
Roll or fold a piece of card into a cone shape.	One person drops a pin onto a table to make a quiet sound.
Try again with different-shaped ear trumpets to find out which one is the best.	The person with the ear trumpet moves away until he or she can only just hear the pin drop.

DEVELOPING SCIENCE LANGUAGE for Physical Processes with 6–7 year year olds

Light and dark

These children tested some different **coloured** fabrics. They wanted to find out which **colour** of coat was best for wearing at **night**. They want to be **safe** when they go out at night. This is what they did.

They cut up squares of different coloured fabric.

They made a hole in the side of a shoe box.

They put a piece of fabric in the shoe box.

They put the lid back on.

They looked through the hole to find out whether they could **see** the fabric. It was quite **dark** inside the box. It was **dim**.

They tried different coloured fabrics to find out which colour they could see most easily.

The **light** fabrics were the easiest to see. They could not see the **black** fabric at all.

They decided that a **white** or yellow coat would be the safest for wearing at night.

Photocopiable

Light and dark

1. What were the children trying to find out? _____
   _____

2. What did they use? Write a list. _____
   _____

3. What did they do to find out which fabric was easiest to see?
   _____

4. Was it dark or light inside the box? _____

5. Why was it dark inside the box? Choose two of these words to use in your answer:

light	dim
dark	black
source	bright

   _____
   _____

6. What happened when they looked at the black fabric in the box? _____
   _____

7. Which colours are best for coats to wear at night-time?
   _____ _____

8. Circle the correct words.

   In a cupboard it is **bright / dim**. In a greenhouse it is **bright / dim**.

   Under the bed covers it is **dark / light**. With a torch it is **dark / light**.

What colour is your coat? Write about going out in your coat at night.

DEVELOPING SCIENCE LANGUAGE for Physical Processes with 6–7 year olds

Light and dark

1. The children wanted to know which colour was safest to wear at _____.

2. Tick the things the children needed. Use the pictures and writing on the 'Light and dark' sheet to help you.

   ☐ a shoe box ☐ paper ☐ sticky tape
   ☐ a ruler ☐ glue ☐ a pen
   ☐ scissors ☐ coloured fabric ☐ paper clips

3. They looked through a _____ in the box to find out whether they could see the _____ .

   To answer the next two questions, circle the correct words.

4. Inside the box it was **quite dark / quite light**. It was **bright / dim**.

5. It was dark inside the box because

   the box was black / the light could not get in.

6. Could they see the black fabric in the box? _____

7. The best colour for a coat to wear at night-time is _____

   or _____ .

8. Circle the correct words.

   In a cupboard it is **bright / dim**. In a greenhouse it is **bright / dim**.

   Under the bed covers it is **dark / light**. With a torch it is **dark / light**.

What colour is your coat? Write about going out in your coat at night.

Light sources

A **light source** is anything that makes light.

Some things are **shiny**. They are not light sources. If you look at them in a dark place, you cannot see them. They look shiny in light places because they **reflect** the light.

Colour in the **light sources**.

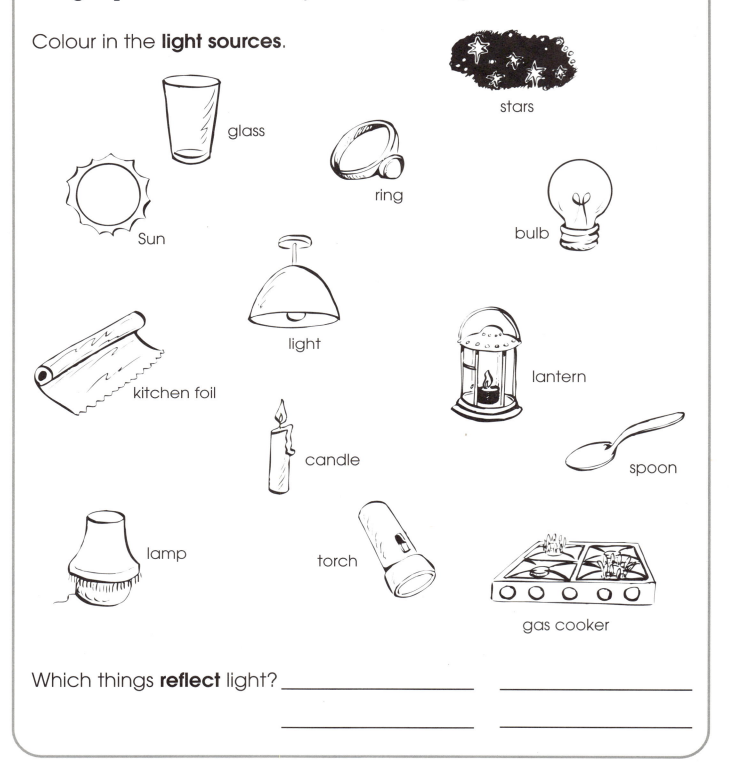

Which things **reflect** light? _____ _____

_____ _____

Warning lights

Some lights give us a **warning**.

Colour in the warning lights in the correct colours.

Cut out these labels. Stick each label next to the correct picture.

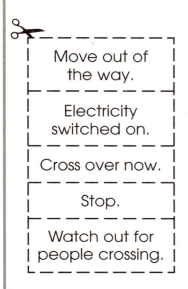

- Move out of the way.
- Electricity switched on.
- Cross over now.
- Stop.
- Watch out for people crossing.

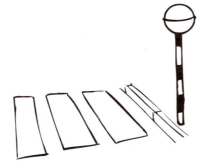

What other lights have you seen that give you a warning or a message? Draw them here.

Photocopiable

Light sources game

Teacher instructions
Photocopy onto card. Cut along the dotted lines. Fold each card in half along the solid line, with the text on the outside, and fasten with adhesive tape.

If you are working with a small group, give each child a card. If you are working with the whole class, share the cards out one between two or three. All the cards must be given out.

The child (or group) with the card marked * reads the question aloud. The child with the answer to that question reads out the answer, then reads out the question on the back of the card. This goes on until the first child has read out the answer on his or her card.

Q	* Something that makes light is called a…	A	no
Q	What light source can you see in the sky in the daytime?	A	light source
Q	What light sources can you see in the sky at night?	A	the Sun
Q	What light source has batteries inside?	A	stars
Q	What light source is made from wax?	A	a torch
Q	How do you light a candle?	A	a candle
Q	When there is no light source it is…	A	with a match
Q	When there is a lot of light we say it is…	A	dark
Q	When there is not much light we say it is…	A	bright
Q	Are shiny things like mirrors light sources?	A	dim

DEVELOPING SCIENCE LANGUAGE for Physical Processes with 6–7 year olds

Day and night

In the **daytime** it is **light**. Often we can see the **Sun** in the daytime. The Sun makes light for us. Even when there are **clouds** in the **sky**, the light from the Sun can get through.

Most animals know the **day** has started when it starts to get light. This is the **morning**, the time when we usually wake up. Birds in the trees start to sing, chickens come out of their sheds, and we wake up.

When it is **midday**, the morning ends. We usually have some lunch around midday. After midday, the **afternoon** starts.

Later on, it is **evening**. It begins to get **dark**, then it gets **darker** and darker. We cannot see the Sun any more. Sometimes we can see the **Moon** and **stars** in the sky. It is **night**. The birds stop singing, the chickens go back into their sheds, and we go to sleep.

Photocopiable

Day and night

1. When is it light? _____

2. Where does the light come from in the daytime? _____

3. When it is cloudy, where is the Sun? _____
   _____

4. How do animals know when it is daytime? _____

5. Do all animals come out in the daytime? _____

6. Can you think of some animals   _____
   or birds that come out at night? _____
                                     _____
                                     _____

7. Put these words in order.

   (afternoon)   (night)   (morning)   (evening)

   _____   _____   _____   _____

8. What happens in the evening?
   _____

9. How do animals and birds know when it is night?
   _____

10. Can you see the Sun at night? _____

11. What can you see in the sky at night?
    _____ and _____

Write a list of questions that the 'Day and night' sheet answers.

DEVELOPING SCIENCE LANGUAGE for Physical Processes with 6–7 year olds

Day and night

1. Draw lines to match the words.

   day   dark
   night   light

2. What can you sometimes see in the sky in the daytime? Tick the correct boxes.

   Moon ☐   Sun ☐
   stars ☐   clouds ☐

3. What gives us light in the daytime? _____

4. Animals know the day has started because it gets _____.

5. When does it begin to get dark? _____

6. Write these words in order.

   afternoon   night   morning   evening

   _____ _____ _____ _____

7. How do chickens know when to go back into their sheds?

   _____

Write a list of questions that the 'Day and night' sheet answers.

Photocopiable

In the sky

Cut out the pictures and the labels. Match the labels to the pictures. Each picture should have one big label and one small label.

| You can see this in the day if it is not cloudy. |
| You can see these at night if it is not cloudy. |
| You can often see this at night. Sometimes you can see it in the evening or early in the morning. |
| These can cover the Moon at night and the Sun in the day. |

| Moon |
| clouds |
| Sun |
| stars |

DEVELOPING SCIENCE LANGUAGE for Physical Processes with 6–7 year olds

Morning, midday, evening and night

Use the words in the box to help you write about each picture.

| day |
| night |
| Sun |
| Moon |
| stars |
| light |
| dim |
| dark |
| morning |
| midday |
| evening |
| bright |

DEVELOPING SCIENCE LANGUAGE for Physical Processes with 6–7 year olds

Day and night dictionary

You need: 'Day and night dictionary (2)', scissors.

1. Fold the sheet in half.

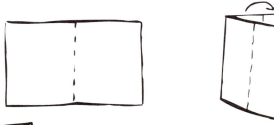

2. Fold it in half again.

3. Fold it in half again.

4. Open it out and fold it like this:

5. Cut from the fold to the bottom.

6. Open the sheet like this:

7. Fold it up so the title is on the front.

8. Write in your dictionary what each word means. You can draw pictures too.

Enlarge to A3 size

Photocopiable

Day and night dictionary

2

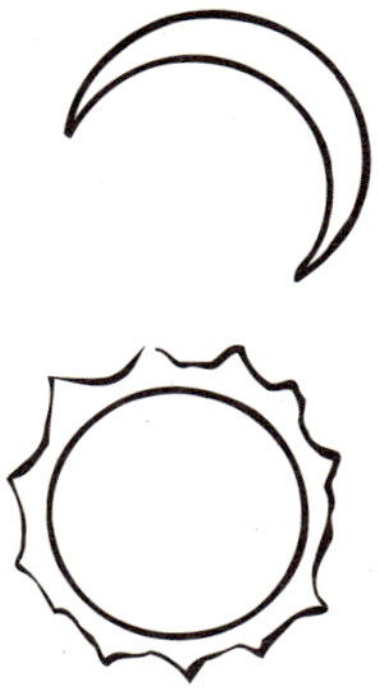

Name: _____

Day and night dictionary

afternoon
The time of day after midday. It is light in the afternoon.

bright

Sun

stars

clouds

dark

night

morning

day

dim

Moon

midday

evening

light

Enlarge to A3 size

DEVELOPING SCIENCE LANGUAGE for Physical Processes with 6–7 year olds

Photocopiable

Shadows in the day and at night

Use the words in the box to help you write about these pictures.

shadow	light	dark	Sun	torch
small	large	block	through	shine
day	night	behind	in front	

When it is light, we can often see shadows. _____

_____
_____
_____
_____

When it is dark, we can use a torch to make shadows. ____

_____
_____
_____
_____
_____
_____

DEVELOPING SCIENCE LANGUAGE for Physical Processes with 6–7 year olds